Table of Cc

CW00631456

chapter **1**   Creativity   7

chapter **2**   Leadership   13

chapter **3**   Teamwork   29

chapter **4**   Deadlines and Time Management   35

chapter **5**   Dedication and Attitude   41

chapter **6**   Personality   45

chapter **7**   Decision Making   55

chapter **8**   Goals   61

chapter **9**   Creative Questions   67

chapter **10** Customer Service   75

chapter **11** Background and Experience   79

chapter **12** Business Skills and Knowledge   87

chapter **13** Communication   93

chapter **14** Job Searching and Scheduling   99

chapter **15** Knowledge of the Company   107

Index   112

Dear Reader,

Thank you for purchasing **HR Interview Questions You'll Most Likely Be Asked.** We are committed to publishing books that are content-rich, concise and approachable enabling more readers to read and make the fullest use of them. We hope this book provides the most enriching learning experience as you prepare for your interview.

Should you have any questions or suggestions, feel free to email us at **reachus@vibrantpublishers.com**

Thanks again for your purchase. Good luck with your interview!

— Vibrant Publishers Team

facebook.com/vibrantpublishers

HR Interview Questions

Review these typical interview questions and think about how you would answer them. Read the answers listed; you will find best possible answers along strategy suggestions with it.

This page is intentionally left blank

Chapter **1**

Creativity

1: Every business faces problems that affect productivity and profitability. Can you share with me a solution you developed for a workplace problem that was unusual or unexpected, and actually led to increased productivity or profitability?

Answer:

The correct answer will provide quantifiable evidence of the candidate's efforts which increased profitability and productivity.

As an example: A customer placed a large order for an item with specifications that were significantly different from the product offered by my company. I needed to meet this customer's needs without creating increased production costs. To satisfy this customer, I worked with company engineers and found a way to modify the production machinery to meet this need without increasing my company's production costs. As part of the engineering process, I was able to implement cost savings through reduced labor costs and better utilization of the required raw materials.

2: Can you describe how you analyzed a workplace problem you have faced, and how your analysis led to the solution?

Answer:

The correct answer should provide evidence of the candidate's analytical skills, and the candidate's ability to look at an issue from different angles and develop the best solution to a problem.

As an example: The employer wanted to ramp up production to three shifts per day to meet increased demand for a product without hiring more than five new employees. I found a way to rearrange the existing employees' schedules without creating significant dissatisfaction. Additionally; I was able to fit the five new employees into the schedule in such a way that they were able to work smoothly together to increase the production.'

3: There are times when customers are unhappy with your company's product or service and expect a solution that is more than what is normally provided. Can you share a time when you were able to provide a solution to an unusual customer expectation that made both customer and management happy?

Answer:

The correct answer should provide insight into the candidate's attitudes towards meeting customer service challenges. The answer should provide evidence of the candidate's willingness to creatively respond to difficult customers without violating company policies.

As an example: An important customer from a different time zone had a need to regularly conduct business outside of my company's normal business hours. I found a way to make a customer service representative available without increasing over time hours. I was able to meet the customer's needs without increasing the financial burden on the company.

4: Describe workplace innovations you have developed on your own initiative.

Answer:

The correct answer should provide tangible evidence of the candidate's willingness to take the initiative to solve problems without being prompted by supervisors.

As an example: My company recorded employee time on paper time cards, and to reduce payroll expenses. I initiated a project to launch fully computerized system. It included reporting payroll taxes and fees to the state and federal governments, and a direct deposit system for the payment of employee salaries. My efforts saved the company thousands of dollars each year in tracking and paying payroll expenses.

5: Describe workplace innovations you helped develop as a member of a team.

Answer:

The correct response to this question will show how the candidate is able to work as a team member.

As an example: I was assigned to a management team with the task of developing an entire new line of interior paint products that included new colors, new textures and competitive retail pricing. I was able to help the team develop a customer survey that when completed showed the team exactly which products customers would desire and would purchase if priced right.

6: Where do you find ideas?

Answer:

Ideas can come from all places, and an interviewer wants to see that your ideas are just as varied. Mention multiple places that you gain ideas from, or settings in which you find yourself brainstorming. Additionally, elaborate on how you record ideas or expand upon them later.

7: How do you achieve creativity in the workplace?

Answer:

It's important to show the interviewer that you're capable of being resourceful and innovative in the workplace, without stepping outside the lines of company values. Explain where ideas normally stem from for you (examples may include an exercise such as list-making or a mind map), and connect this to a particular task in your job that it would be helpful to be creative in.

8: How do you push others to create ideas?

Answer:

If you're in a supervisory position, this may be requiring employees to submit a particular number of ideas, or to complete regular idea-generating exercises, in order to work their creative muscles. However, you can also push others around you to create ideas simply by creating more of your own. Additionally, discuss

with the interviewer the importance of questioning people as a
way to inspire ideas and change.

9: Describe your creativity.

Answer:

Try to keep this answer within the professional realm, but if you
have an impressive background in something creative outside of
your employment history, don't be afraid to include it in your
answer also. The best answers about creativity will relate
problem-solving skills, goal-setting, and finding innovative ways
to tackle a project or make a sale in the workplace. However,
passions outside of the office are great, too (so long as they don't
cut into your work time or mental space).

This page is intentionally left blank

Chapter **2**

Leadership

10: Was there a time you were called upon to reorganize your department? If so, what steps did you take to ensure the reorganization was successful?

Answer:

The candidate should be able to relate to a verifiable time when she was asked to reorganize her department. The correct answer should say something like, "just last year my company decided there should be reorganization program because the internet had significantly changed the way we were doing business."

As an example: My first step was to identify the exact business functions that were driving the need for change. Secondly, I identified the functions that were working properly and should not be changed. Thirdly, I made a determination of how the people in the department needed to be reassigned to best accomplish the reorganization. In the end, the reorganization was successful, and the company's profits were increased.

11: Tell me about a time when you led a team to successfully complete a project.

Answer:

The correct answer should describe a real situation in which the candidate led his team to complete a project.

As an example: Last year my management team was assigned the task of finding a way to improve our company's overall customer service rating. We were having trouble finding and retaining customer service representatives that were responsive to the needs of our customers. Through customer service surveys and close observation of customer service interactions, we were able to identify a number of customer service representatives that were providing outstanding service to our customers. We assigned these people as trainers and mentors for the purpose of motivating the entire staff to provide a high level of service to our customers.

12: Describe a time when you played a major leadership role in a special event.

Answer:

To answer this question correctly, the candidate should be able to describe an actual event in which she was the primary leader. The special event could be a job fair, awards banquet, marketing meeting or other event.

As an example: Our Company is constantly looking for talented people. We feel the greatest competitive advantage we have is our people. In April last year, I was given the responsibility to set up a regional job fair designed to attract college graduates. The job fair was a total success. We had over 1000 recent college graduates come to the job fair. Our human resources people were able to fill all of our open positions.

13: How have the people around you responded to your leadership efforts?

Answer:

The expected answer from the candidate is the people he was leading responded very well to his leadership efforts. The candidate should be able to provide solid evidence that people respond to him in a positive manner.

As an example: For my efforts over the last year to increase my department's sales performance, I received the highest recognition the company provides. The people working in my department responded in an overwhelmingly positive manner to the programs I installed. My department was able to improve sales performance by 15 percent.

14: Describe your strengths as a leader.

Answer:

To answer this question correctly, the candidate should be able to describe the elements of his leadership style that makes him a great leader.

As an example: One of my greatest strengths as a leader is my ability to motivate people to accomplish tasks they felt were too difficult for them. Recently I worked with a team to overhaul the way we handled incoming shipments. We have many deliveries come in throughout the day, and our efforts to handle the work load were strained to the limit. Working together, we developed a work schedule that maximized the number of people we had available to meet peak workload requirements.

15: Describe the greatest weakness in your leadership style.

Answer:

The candidate should answer this question in an honest and open manner. It is hard for some people to admit any weakness, making this question a great indicator of the candidate's willingness to be transparent.

As an example: There are times I am not as observant as I should be. While working on a project earlier this year, I failed to see that an important element of the plan had been done incorrectly. My error caused us to miss an important deadline. I am working very hard to improve my observation skills.

16: If a group of people in your department were talking about you behind your back, what do you think they would be saying about you?

Answer:

The candidate may be reluctant to venture and answer for this question, nevertheless the interviewer should press for an answer. This question should shed significant light on the candidate's self-image.

As an example: I have noticed on occasions that my actions cause some interesting conversations throughout my department. It is hard for me to ignore what is being said. Some people say that I cater to the boss's whims in an effort to get my name at the top of the promotion list. All I am concerned about is doing the best job that I can. I can't control what other people say about me.

17: Describe a difficult project that required you to build consensus on a divisive issue.

Answer:

Some candidates may consider this a difficult question to answer. Although it is difficult, the interviewer is looking for the candidate to reveal how he deals with divisiveness in the workplace.

As an example: We had a project to complete that was so large it required the work of three departments. Right in the middle of the project, a serious dispute arose over which department would take the lead position on the project. Tempers became very hot because of the political infighting. Through many hours of painstaking negotiation, I helped everyone involved find a way to put their best foot forward and receive the recognition they were looking for.

18: Describe a project or task that required you to develop agreement or cooperation between departments.

Answer:

The candidate should be able to provide tangible evidence that she is able to work with other leaders to get important work accomplished.

As an example: We had a project to improve the wheel bearings on the tricycles our company sells. My department was in charge of the bearings, and another department was in charge of developing the new wheels that would be used on the tricycle. It took significant interdepartmental cooperation to get the bearings and wheels to the correct size for each model of tricycle the company sold.

19: Describe a situation when you needed to build support within your department for an idea you thought would greatly benefit your company.

Answer:

To answer this question correctly, the candidate should describe a situation which required him to build support for his vision and make his ideas become a reality.

As an example: I had this idea of finding a way to get the company to develop a child care center in our building. It would be very convenient for people with small children who worked in the building. The initial start-up costs would be significant, but the long-term benefits in increased productivity would pay for the project. It took me almost two years to make my idea become a reality, but everyone in the company is very happy the child care center is in operation.

20: Would you rather receive more authority or more responsibility at work?

Answer:

There are pros and cons to each of these options, and your interviewer will be more interested to see that you can provide a critical answer to the question. Receiving more authority may mean greater decision-making power and may be great for those with outstanding leadership skills, while greater responsibility may be a growth opportunity for those looking to advance steadily throughout their careers.

21: What do you do when someone in a group isn't contributing their fair share?

Answer:

This is a particularly important question if you're interviewing for a position in a supervisory role - explain the ways in which you would identify the problem, and how you would go about pulling aside the individual to discuss their contributions. It's important to understand the process of creating a dialogue, so that you can communicate your expectations clearly to the individual, give them a chance to respond, and to make clear what needs to change. After this, create an action plan with the group member to ensure their contributions are on par with others in the group.

22: Tell me about a time when you made a decision that was outside of your authority.

Answer:

While an answer to this question may portray you as being decisive and confident, it could also identify you to an employer as a potential problem employee. Instead, it may be best to slightly refocus the question into an example of a time that you took on additional responsibilities, and thus had to make decisions that were outside of your normal authority (but which had been granted to you in the specific instance). Discuss how the weight of the decision affected your decision-making process, and the outcomes of the situation.

23: Are you comfortable going to supervisors with disputes?

Answer:

If a problem arises, employers want to know that you will handle it in a timely and appropriate manner. Emphasize that you've rarely had disputes with supervisors in the past, but if a situation were to arise, you feel perfectly comfortable in discussing it with the person in question in order to find a resolution that is satisfactory to both parties.

24: If you had been in charge at your last job, what would you have done differently?

Answer:

No matter how many ideas you have about how things could run better, or opinions on the management at your previous job, remain positive when answering this question. It's okay to show thoughtful reflection on how something could be handled in order to increase efficiency or improve sales but be sure to keep all of your suggestions focused on making things better, rather than talking about ways to eliminate waste or negativity.

25: Do you believe employers should praise or reward employees for a job well done?

Answer:

Recognition is always great after completing a difficult job, but there are many employers who may ask this question as a way to infer as to whether or not you'll be a high-maintenance worker. While you may appreciate rewards or praise, it's important to convey to the interviewer that you don't require accolades to be confident that you've done your job well. If you are interviewing for a supervisory position where you would be the one praising other employees, highlight the importance of praise in boosting team morale.

26: What do you believe is the most important quality a leader can have?

Answer:

There are many important skills for a leader to have in any business, and the most important component of this question is that you explain why the quality you choose to highlight is important. Try to choose a quality such as communication skills, or an ability to inspire people, and relate it to a specific instance in which you displayed the quality among a team of people.

27: Tell me about a time when an unforeseen problem arose. How did you handle it?

Answer:

It's important that you are resourceful, and level-headed under pressure. An interviewer wants to see that you handle problems systematically, and that you can deal with change in an orderly process. Outline the situation clearly, including all solutions and results of the process you implemented.

28: Can you give me an example of a time when you were able to improve *X objective* at your previous job?

Answer:

It's important here to focus on an improvement you made that created tangible results for your company. Increasing efficiency is certainly a very important element in business, but employers are also looking for concrete results such as increased sales or cut expenses. Explain your process thoroughly, offering specific numbers and evidence wherever possible, particularly in outlining the results.

29: Tell me about a time when a supervisor did not provide specific enough direction on a project.

Answer:

While many employers want their employees to follow very specific guidelines without much decision-making power, it's important also to be able to pick up a project with vague direction and to perform self-sufficiently. Give examples of necessary questions that you asked and specify how you determined whether a question was something you needed to ask of a supervisor or whether it was something you could determine on your own.

30: Tell me about a time when you were in charge of leading a project.

Answer:

Lead the interviewer through the process of the project, just as you would have with any of your team members. Explain the goal of the project, the necessary steps, and how you delegated tasks to your team. Include the results, and what you learned as a result of the leadership opportunity.

31: Tell me about a suggestion you made to a former employer that was later implemented.

Answer:

Employers want to see that you're interested in improving your company and doing your part - offer a specific example of something you did to create a positive change in your previous job. Explain how you thought of the idea, how your supervisors received it, and what other employees thought was the idea was put into place.

32: Tell me about a time when you thought of a way something in the workplace could be done more efficiently.

Answer:

Focus on the positive aspects of your idea. It's important not to portray your old company or boss negatively, so doesn't elaborate on how inefficient a particular system was. Rather, explain a situation in which you saw an opportunity to increase productivity or to streamline a process, and explain in a general step-by-step how you implemented a better system.

33: Is there a difference between leading and managing people - which is your greater strength?

Answer:

There is a difference - leaders are often great idea people, passionate, charismatic, and with the ability to organize and inspire others, while managers are those who ensure a system runs, facilitate its operations, make authoritative decisions, and who take great responsibility for all aspects from overall success to the finest decisions. Consider which of these is most applicable to the position, and explain how you fit into this role, offering concrete examples of your past experience.

34: Do you function better in a leadership role, or as a worker on a team?

Answer:

It is important to consider what qualities the interviewer is looking for in your position, and to express how you embody this role. If you're a leader, highlight your great ideas, drive and passion, and ability to incite others around you to action. If you work great in teams, focus on your dedication to the task at hand, your cooperation and communication skills, and your ability to keep things running smoothly.

35: Tell me about a time when you discovered something in the workplace that was disrupting your (or others) productivity - what did you do about it.

Answer:

Try to not focus on negative aspects of your previous job too much, but instead choose an instance in which you found a positive, and quick, solution to increase productivity. Focus on the way you noticed the opportunity, how you presented a solution to your supervisor, and then how the change was implemented (most importantly, talk about how you led the change initiative). This is a great opportunity for you to display your problem-solving skills, as well as your resourceful nature and leadership skills.

36: How do you perform in a job with clearly-defined objectives and goals?

Answer:

It is important to consider the position when answering this question - clearly, it is best if you can excel in a job with clearly-defined objectives and goals (particularly if you're in an entry level or sales position). However, if you're applying for a position with a leadership role or creative aspect to it, be sure to focus on the ways that you additionally enjoy the challenges of developing and implementing your own ideas.

37: How do you perform in a job where you have great decision.making power?

Answer:

The interviewer wants to know that, if hired, you won't be the type of employee who needs constant supervision or who asks for advice, authority, or feedback every step of the way. Explain that you work well in a decisive, productive environment, and that you look forward to taking initiative in your position.

38: If you saw another employee doing something dishonest or unethical, what would you do?

Answer:

In the case of witnessing another employee doing something dishonest, it is always best to act in accordance with company policies for such a situation - and if you don't know what this company's specific policies are, feel free to simply state that you would handle it according to the policy and by reporting it to the appropriate persons in charge. If you are aware of the company's policies (such as if you are seeking a promotion within your own company), it is best to specifically outline your actions according to the policy.

39: Tell me about a time when you learned something on your own that later helped in your professional life.

Answer:

This question is important because it allows the interviewer to gain insight into your dedication to learning and advancement.

Choose an example solely from your personal life, and provide a brief anecdote ending in the lesson you learned. Then, explain in a clear and thorough manner how this lesson has translated into a usable skill or practice in your position.

40: Tell me about a time when you developed a project idea at work.

Answer:

Choose a project idea that you developed that was typical of projects you might complete in the new position. Outline where your idea came from, the type of research you did to ensure its success and relevancy, steps that were included in the project, and the end results. Offer specific before and after statistics, to show its success.

41: Tell me about a time when you took a risk on a project.

Answer:

Whether the risk involved something as complex as taking on a major project with limited resources or time, or simply volunteering for a task that was outside your field of experience, show that you are willing to stretch out of your comfort zone and to try new things. Offer specific examples of why something you did was risky and explain what you learned in the process - or how this prepared you for a job objective you later faced in your career.

42: What would you tell someone who was looking to get into this field?

Answer:

This question allows you to be the expert - and will show the interviewer that you have the knowledge and experience to go along with any training and education on your resume. Offer your knowledge as advice of unexpected things that someone entering the field may encounter and be sure to end with positive advice such as the passion or dedication to the work that is required to truly succeed.

This page is intentionally left blank

Chapter 3

Teamwork

43: How would you handle a negative coworker?

Answer:

Everyone has to deal with negative coworkers - and the single best way to do so is to remain positive. You may try to build a relationship with the coworker or relate to them in some way, but even if your efforts are met with a cold shoulder, you must retain your positive attitude. Above all, stress that you would never allow a coworker's negativity to impact your own work or productivity.

44: What would you do if you witnessed a coworker surfing the web, reading a book, etc, wasting company time?

Answer:

The interviewer will want to see that you realize how detrimental it is for employees to waste company time, and that it is not something you take lightly. Explain the way you would adhere to company policy, whether that includes talking to the coworker yourself, reporting the behavior straight to a supervisor, or talking to someone in HR.

45: How do you handle competition among yourself and other employees?

Answer:

Healthy competition can be a great thing, and it is best to stay focused on the positive aspects of this here. Don't bring up conflict among yourself and other coworkers, and instead focus on the motivation to keep up with the great work of others, and the ways in which coworkers may be a great support network in helping to push you to new successes.

46: When is it okay to socialize with co-workers?

Answer:

This question has two extreme answers (all the time, or never), and your interviewer, in most cases, will want to see that you fall somewhere in the middle. It's important to establish solid relationships with your coworkers, but never at the expense of getting work done. Ideally, relationship-building can happen with exercises of teamwork and special projects, as well as in the break room.

47: Tell me about a time when a major change was made at your last job, and how you handled it.

Answer:

Provide a set-up for the situation including the old system, what the change was, how it was implemented, and the results of the change, and include how you felt about each step of the way. Be sure that your initial thoughts on the old system are neutral, and that your excitement level grows with each step of the new change, as an interviewer will be pleased to see your adaptability.

48: When delegating tasks, how do you choose which tasks go to which team members?

Answer:

The interviewer is looking to gain insight into your thought process with this question, so be sure to offer thorough reasoning behind your choice. Explain that you delegate tasks based on each individual's personal strengths, or that you look at how many other projects each person is working on at the time, in order to create the best fit possible.

49: Tell me about a time when you had to stand up for something you believed strongly about to coworkers or a supervisor.

Answer:

While it may be difficult to explain a situation of conflict to an interviewer, this is a great opportunity to display your passions and convictions, and your dedication to your beliefs. Explain not just the situation to the interviewer, but also elaborate on why it was so important to you to stand up for the issue, and how your coworker or supervisor responded to you afterward - were they more respectful? Unreceptive? Open-minded? Apologetic?

50: Tell me about a time when you helped someone finish their work, even though it wasn't "your job."

Answer:

Though you may be frustrated when required to pick up someone else's slack, it's important that you remain positive about lending a hand. The interviewer will be looking to see if you're a team player, and by helping someone else finish a task that he or she couldn't manage alone, you show both your willingness to help the team succeed, and your own competence.

51: What are the challenges of working on a team? How do you handle this?

Answer:

There are many obvious challenges to working on a team, such as handling different perspectives, navigating individual schedules, or accommodating difficult workers. It's best to focus on one challenge, such as individual team members missing deadlines or failing to keep commitments, and then offer a solution that clearly addresses the problem. For example, you could organize weekly status meetings for your team to discuss progress or assign shorter deadlines in order to keep the long-term deadline on schedule.

52: Do you value diversity in the workplace?

Answer:

Diversity is important in the workplace in order to foster an environment that is accepting, equalizing, and full of different perspectives and backgrounds. Be sure to show your awareness of these issues and stress the importance of learning from others' experiences.

53: How would you handle a situation in which a coworker was not accepting of someone else's diversity?

Answer:

Explain that it is important to adhere to company policies regarding diversity, and that you would talk to the relevant supervisors or management team. When it is appropriate, it could also be best to talk to the coworker in question about the benefits of alternate perspectives - if you can handle the situation yourself, it's best not to bring resolvable issues to management.

54: Are you rewarded more from working on a team, or accomplishing a task on your own?

Answer:

It's best to show a balance between these two aspects - your employer wants to see that you're comfortable working on your own, and that you can complete tasks efficiently and well without assistance. However, it's also important for your employer to see that you can be a team player, and that you understand the value that multiple perspectives and efforts can bring to a project.

This page is intentionally left blank

Chapter **4**

Deadlines and Time Management

55: Tell me about a time when you didn't meet a deadline.

Answer:

Ideally, this hasn't happened - but if it has, make sure you use a minor example to illustrate the situation, emphasize how long ago it happened, and be sure that you did as much as you could to ensure that the deadline was met. Additionally, be sure to include what you learned about managing time better or prioritizing tasks in order to meet all future deadlines.

56: How do you eliminate distractions while working?

Answer:

With the increase of technology and the ease of communication, new distractions arise every day. Your interviewer will want to see that you are still able to focus on work, and that your productivity has not been affected, by an example showing a routine you employ in order to stay on task.

57: Tell me about a time when you worked in a position with a weekly or monthly quota to meet. How often were you successful?

Answer:

Your numbers will speak for themselves, and you must answer this question honestly. If you were regularly met your quotas, be sure to highlight this in a confident manner and don't be shy in pointing out your strengths in this area. If your statistics are less than stellar, try to point out trends in which they increased toward the end of your employment, and show reflection as to ways you can improve in the future.

58: Tell me about a time when you met a tough deadline, and how you were able to complete it.

Answer:

Explain how you were able to prioritize tasks, or to delegate portions of an assignments to other team members, in order to deal with a tough deadline. It may be beneficial to specify why the deadline was tough - make sure it's clear that it was not a result of procrastination on your part. Finally, explain how you were able to successfully meet the deadline, and what it took to get there in the end.

59: How do you stay organized when you have multiple projects on your plate?

Answer:

The interviewer will be looking to see that you can manage your time and work well - and being able to handle multiple projects at once, and still giving each the attention it deserves, is a great mark of a worker's competence and efficiency. Go through a typical process of goal-setting and prioritizing, and explain the steps of these to the interviewer, so he or she can see how well you manage time.

60: How much time during your work day do you spend on "auto-pilot?"

Answer:

While you may wonder if the employer is looking to see how efficient you are with this question (for example, so good at your job that you don't have to think about it), but in almost every case, the employer wants to see that you're constantly thinking, analyzing, and processing what's going on in the workplace. Even if things are running smoothly, there's usually an opportunity somewhere to make things more efficient or to increase sales or productivity. Stress your dedication to ongoing development and convey that being on "auto-pilot" is not conducive to that type of success.

61: How do you handle deadlines?

Answer:

The most important part of handling tough deadlines is to prioritize tasks and set goals for completion, as well as to delegate or eliminate unnecessary work. Lead the interviewer through a general scenario and display your competency through your ability to organize and set priorities, and most importantly, remain calm.

62: Tell me about your personal problem-solving process.

Answer:

Your personal problem-solving process should include outlining the problem, coming up with possible ways to fix the problem, and setting a clear action plan that leads to resolution. Keep your answer brief and organized, and explain the steps in a concise, calm manner that shows you are level-headed even under stress.

63: What sort of things at work can make you stressed?

Answer:

As it's best to stay away from negatives, keep this answer brief and simple. While answering that nothing at work makes you stressed will not be very believable to the interviewer, keep your answer to one generic principle such as when members of a team don't keep their commitments, and then focus on a solution you generally employ to tackle that stress, such as having weekly status meetings or intermittent deadlines along the course of a project.

64: What do you look like when you are stressed about something? How do you solve it?

Answer:

This is a trick question - your interviewer wants to hear that you don't look any different when you're stressed, and that you don't allow negative emotions to interfere with your productivity. As far as how you solve your stress, it's best if you have a simple solution mastered, such as simply taking deep breaths and counting to 10 to bring yourself back to the task at hand.

65: Can you multi-task?

Answer:

Some people can, and some people can't. The most important part of multi-tasking is to keep a clear head at all times about what needs to be done, and what priority each task falls under. Explain how you evaluate tasks to determine priority, and how you manage your time in order to ensure that all are completed efficiently.

66: How many hours per week do you work?

Answer:

Many people get tricked by this question, thinking that answering more hours is better - however, this may cause an employer to wonder why you have to work so many hours in order to get the work done that other people can do in a shorter amount of time. Give a fair estimate of hours that it should take you to complete a job and explain that you are also willing to work extra whenever needed.

67: How many times per day do you check your email?

Answer:

While an employer wants to see that you are plugged into modern technology, it is also important that the number of times you check your email per day is relatively low - perhaps two to three times per day (dependent on the specific field you're in). Checking email is often a great distraction in the workplace, and while it is important to remain connected, much correspondence can simply be handled together in the morning and afternoon.

Chapter **5**

Dedication and Attitude

68: Tell me about a time when you worked additional hours to finish a project.

Answer:

It's important for your employer to see that you are dedicated to your work, and willing to put in extra hours when required or when a job calls for it. However, be careful when explaining why you were called to work additional hours - for instance, did you have to stay late because you set goals poorly earlier in the process? Or on a more positive note, were you working additional hours because a client requested for a deadline to be moved up on short notice? Stress your competence and willingness to give 110% every time.

69: Tell me about a time when your performance exceeded the duties and requirements of your job.

Answer:

If you're a great candidate for the position, this should be an easy question to answer - choose a time when you truly went above and beyond the call of duty and put in additional work or voluntarily took on new responsib-ilities. Remain humble, and express gratitude for the learning opportunity, as well as confidence in your ability to give a repeat performance.

70: What is your driving attitude about work?

Answer:

There are many possible good answers to this question, and the interviewer primarily wants to see that you have a great passion for the job and that you will remain motivated in your career if hired. Some specific driving forces behind your success may include hard work, opportunity, growth potential, or success.

71: Do you take work home with you?

Answer:

It is important to first clarify that you are always willing to take work home when necessary, but you want to emphasize as well that it has not been an issue for you in the past. Highlight skills such as time management, goal-setting, and multi-tasking, which can all ensure that work is completed at work.

72: Describe a typical work day to me.

Answer:

There are several important components in your typical work day, and an interviewer may derive meaning from any or all of them, as well as from your ability to systematically lead him or her through the day. Start at the beginning of your day and proceed chronologically, making sure to emphasize steady productivity, time for review, goal-setting, and prioritizing, as well as some additional time to account for unexpected things that may arise.

73: Tell me about a time when you went out of your way at your previous job.

Answer:

Here it is best to use a specific example of the situation that required you to go out of your way, what your specific position would have required that you did, and how you went above that. Use concrete details, and be sure to include the results, as well as reflection on what you learned in the process.

74: Are you open to receiving feedback and criticisms on your job performance, and adjusting as necessary?

Answer:

This question has a pretty clear answer - yes - but you'll need to display knowledge as to why this is important. Receiving feedback and criticism is one thing, but the most important part of that process is to then implement it into your daily work. Keep a good attitude, and express that you always appreciate constructive feedback.

75: What inspires you?

Answer:

You may find inspiration in nature, reading success stories, or mastering a difficult task, but it's important that your inspiration is positively-based and that you're able to listen and tune into it when it appears. Keep this answer generally based in the professional world, but where applicable, it may stretch a bit into creative exercises in your personal life that, in turn, help you in achieving career objectives.

76: How do you inspire others?

Answer:

This may be a difficult question, as it is often hard to discern the effects of inspiration in others. Instead of offering a specific example of a time when you inspired someone, focus on general principles such as leading by example that you employ in your professional life. If possible, relate this to a quality that someone who inspired you possessed, and discuss the way you have modified or modeled it in your own work.

Chapter 6

Personality

77: What has been your biggest success?

Answer:

Your biggest success should be something that was especially meaningful to you, and that you can talk about passionately - your interviewer will be able to see this. Always have an answer prepared for this question, and be sure to explain how you achieved success, as well as what you learned from the experience.

78: What motivates you?

Answer:

It's best to focus on a key aspect of your work that you can target as a "driving force" behind your everyday work. Whether it's customer service, making a difference, or the chance to further your skills and gain experience, it's important that the interviewer can see the passion you hold for your career and the dedication you have to the position.

79: What do you do when you lose motivation?

Answer:

The best candidates will answer that they rarely lose motivation, because they already employ strategies to keep themselves inspired, and because they remain dedicated to their objectives. Additionally, you may impress the interviewer by explaining that you are motivated by achieving goals and advancing, so small successes are always a great way to regain momentum.

80: What do you like to do in your free time?

Answer:

What you do answer here is not nearly as important as what you don't answer - your interviewer does not want to hear that you like to drink, party, or revel in the nightlife. Instead, choose a few activities to focus on that are greater signs of stability and maturity, and that will not detract from your ability to show up to work and be productive, such as reading, cooking, or photography. This is also a great opportunity to show your interviewer that you are a well-rounded, interesting, and dynamic personality that they would be happy to hire.

81: What sets you apart from other workers?

Answer:

This question is a great opportunity to highlight the specific skill sets and passion you bring to the company that no one else can. If you can't outline exactly what sets you apart from other workers, how will the interviewer see it? Be prepared with a thorough outline of what you will bring to the table, in order to help the company, achieve their goals.

82: Why are you the best candidate for that position?

Answer:

Have a brief response prepared in advance for this question, as this is another very common theme in interviews (variations of the question include: "Why should I hire you, above Candidate B?" and "What can you bring to our company that Candidate B cannot?"). Make sure that your statement does not sound rehearsed and highlight your most unique qualities that show the interviewer why he or she must hire you above all the other candidates. Include specific details about your experience and special projects or recognition you've received that set you apart, and show your greatest passion, commitment, and enthusiasm for the position.

83: What does it take to be successful?

Answer:

Hard work, passion, motivation, and a dedication to learning - these are all potential answers to the ambiguous concept of success. It doesn't matter so much which of these values you choose as the primary means to success, or if you choose a combination of them. It is, however, absolutely key that whichever value you choose, you must clearly display in your attitude, experience, and goals.

84: What would be the biggest challenge in this position for you?

Answer:

Keep this answer positive and remain focused on the opportunities for growth and learning that the position can provide. Be sure that no matter what the challenge is, it's obvious that you're ready and enthusiastic to tackle it, and that you have a full awareness of what it will take to get the job done.

85: Would you describe yourself as an introvert or an extrovert?

Answer:

There are beneficial qualities to each of these, and your answer may depend on what type of work you're involved in. However, a successful leader may be an introvert or extrovert, and similarly, solid team members may also be either. The important aspect of this question is to have the level of self-awareness required to accurately describe yourself.

86: What are some positive character traits that you don't possess?

Answer:

If an interviewer asks you a tough question about your weaknesses, or lack of positive traits, it's best to keep your answer light-hearted and simple - for instance, express your great confidence in your own abilities, followed by a (rather humble) admittance that you could occasionally do to be humbler.

87: What is the greatest lesson you've ever learned?

Answer:

While this is a very broad question, the interviewer will be more interested in hearing what kind of emphasis you place on this value. Your greatest lesson may tie in with something a mentor, parent, or professor once told you, or you may have gleaned it from a book written by a leading expert in your field. Regardless of what the lesson is, it is most important that you can offer an example of how you've incorporated it into your life.

88: Have you ever been in a situation where one of your strengths became a weakness in an alternate setting?

Answer:

It's important to show an awareness of yourself by having an answer for this question, but you want to make sure that the weakness is relatively minor, and that it would still remain a strength in most settings. For instance, you may be an avid reader who reads anything and everything you can find but reading billboards while driving to work may be a dangerous idea.

89: Who has been the most influential person in your life?

Answer:

Give a specific example (and name) to the person who has influenced your life greatly and offer a relevant anecdote about a meaningful exchange the two of you shared. It's great if their influence relates to your professional life, but this particular question opens up the possibility to discuss inspiration in your personal life as well. The interviewer wants to see that you're able to make strong connections with other individuals, and to work under the guiding influence of another person.

90: Do you consider yourself to be a "detailed" or "big picture" type of person?

Answer:

Both of these are great qualities, and it's best if you can incorporate each into your answer. Choose one as your primary type and relate it to experience or specific items from your resume. Then, explain how the other type fits into your work as well.

91: What is your greatest fear?

Answer:

Disclosing your greatest fear openly and without embarrassment is a great way to show your confidence to an employer. Choose a fear that you are clearly doing work to combat, such as a fear of failure that will seem impossible to the interviewer for someone such as yourself, with such clear goals and actions plans outlined. As tempting as it may be to stick with an easy answer such as spiders, stay away from these, as they don't really tell the interviewer anything about yourself that's relevant.

92: What sort of challenges do you enjoy?

Answer:

The challenges you enjoy should demonstrate some sort of initiative or growth potential on your part and should also be in line with your career objectives. Employers will evaluate consistency here, as they analyze critically how the challenges you look forward to are related to your ultimate goals.

93: Tell me about a time you were embarrassed. How did you handle it?

Answer:

No one wants to bring up times they were embarrassed in a job interview, and it's probably best to avoid an anecdote here. However, don't shy away from offering a brief synopsis, followed by a display of your ability to laugh it off. Show the interviewer that it was not an event that impacted you significantly.

94: What is your greatest weakness?

Answer:

This is another one of the most popular questions asked in job interviews, so you should be prepared with an answer already. Try to come up with a weakness that you have that can actually be a strength in an alternate setting - such as, "I'm very detail-oriented and like to ensure that things are done correctly, so I sometimes have difficulty in delegating tasks to others." However, don't try to mask obvious weaknesses - if you have little practical experience in the field, mention that you're looking forward to great opportunities to further your knowledge.

95: What are the three best adjectives to describe you in a work setting?

Answer:

While these three adjectives probably already appear somewhere on your resume, don't be afraid to use them again in order to highlight your best qualities. This is a chance for you to sell yourself to the interviewer, and to point out traits you possess that other candidates do not. Use the most specific and accurate words you can think of and elaborate shortly on how you embody each.

96: What are the three best adjectives to describe you in your personal life?

Answer:

Ideally, the three adjectives that describe you in your personal life should be similar to the adjectives that describe you in your professional life. Employers appreciate consistency, and while they may be understanding of you having an alternate personality outside of the office, it's best if you employ similar principles in your actions both on and off the clock.

97: What type of worker are you?

Answer:

This is an opportunity for you to highlight some of your greatest assets. Characterize some of your talents such as dedicated, self-motivated, detail-oriented, passionate, hard-working, analytical, or customer service focused. Stay away from your weaker qualities here and remain on the target of all the wonderful things that you can bring to the company.

98: Tell me about your happiest day at work.

Answer:

Your happiest day at work should include one of your greatest professional successes, and how it made you feel. Stay focused on what you accomplished and be sure to elaborate on how rewarding or satisfying the achievement was for you.

99: Tell me about your worst day at work.

Answer:

It may have been the worst day ever because of all the mistakes you made, or because you'd just had a huge argument with your best friend, but make sure to keep this answer professionally focused. Try to use an example in which something uncontrollable happened in the workplace (such as an important member of a team quit unexpectedly, which ruined your team's meeting with a client), and focus on the frustration of not being in control of the situation. Keep this answer brief and be sure to end with a reflection on what you learned from the day.

100: What are you passionate about?

Answer:

Keep this answer professionally-focused where possible, but it may also be appropriate to discuss personal issues you are passionate about as well (such as the environment or volunteering at a soup kitchen). Stick to issues that are non-controversial and allow your passion to shine through as you explain what inspires you about the topic and how you stay actively engaged in it. Additionally, if you choose a personal passion, make sure it is one that does not detract from your availability to work or to be productive.

101: What is the piece of criticism you receive most often?

Answer:

An honest, candid answer to this question can greatly impress an interviewer (when, of course, it is coupled with an explanation of what you're doing to improve), but make sure the criticism is something minimal or unrelated to your career.

102: What type of work environment do you succeed the most in?

Answer:

Be sure to research the company and the specific position before heading into the interview. Tailor your response to fit the job you'd be working in and explain why you enjoy that type of environment over others. However, it's also extremely important to be adaptable, so remain flexible to other environments as well.

103: Are you an emotional person?

Answer:

It's best to focus on your positive emotions - passion, happiness, motivations - and to stay away from other extreme emotions that may cause you to appear unbalanced. While you want to display your excitement for the job, be sure to remain level-headed and cool at all times, so that the interviewer knows you're not the type of person who lets emotions take you over and get in the way of your work.

Chapter **7**

Decision Making

104: Have you come across any decision-making situations in the past?

Answer:

The interviewer offers you a chance to share your experiences and it's your turn to grab this opportunity and impress the interviewer. You must answer prioritizing the fact that decision-making is the most essential part in managing any organization. Highlight situations and incidents where you had to take important decisions carefully and consciously after consulting higher officials and you need to make sure that you hold hand of the interviewer and take him through your experiences in an imagery manner.

105: How will you make decisions under pressure?

Answer:

The first step you should do is prioritizing issues. This will help you to take up the most important problem first. Communicate in a calm and confident manner and use cues from your experience to find solutions. If the problem is complex, don't just depend on your intuition but also consult those who are closest to the ground in managing the problem.

106: Do you think it is always important to make ethically correct decisions?

Answer:

You should know that opportunistic decisions are short lived. Ethics should be the foundation of every business and absence of it could lead to legal concerns. Violations of ethical principles can cost any business organization. These together imply responsible decision-making.

107: Does your emotional maturity play a role in making decisions?

Answer:

A leader's emotional maturity does play a role while making decisions. You should always keep your decisions simple, balanced and rational and never let emotions come in the way. You must be resistant from being swayed away by any desired outcome.

108: According to you, decision-making should be done by the manager or by a team?

Answer

Decision-making can be done either by the manager or by a team; it entirely depends upon the type of problem. The manager must allow the group members to share their views if the problem needs to be handled with expert assistance. Ultimately the final decision must be taken by the manager himself after considering all the possibilities.

109: Good business decisions are based on sound empirical evidence. Do you agree with this view?

Answer:

Intuitions are useful during threatening situations, but rational decisions become even more reliable when made on strong empirical evidence. Hence, this view is indeed right.

110: When do you think a team can be involved in decision-making?

Answer:

A problem which arises at the team level must be discussed by all the team members in order to identify a suitable solution for the problem. The manager's experiences can be called for if necessary.

111: Do you think decision-making is a form of planning? If yes, what is the similarity between the two?

Answer:

Yes, decision-making is no doubt a form of planning. As in

planning, decision-making also affects a future course of action and involves choosing from alternatives. Planning, along with its procedures, policies and objectives, is an outcome of decision-making.

112: In a financial services company like ours how do you think decisions should be made?

Answer:

The decisions should be arrived after deep analysis of the hard data and not merely based on your personal instincts, which may lead to disaster.

113: What are the steps to be followed in attaining a decision?

Answer:

The steps to be followed in order to arrive at a decision include problem recognition, problem analysis, finding various alternatives to solve the problem, selecting the best alternative and finally applying and verifying it for the best result possible.

114: How do you make decisions?

Answer:

This is a great opportunity for you to wow your interviewer with your decisiveness, confidence, and organizational skills. Make sure that you outline a process for decision-making, and that you stress the importance of weighing your options, as well as in trusting intuition. If you answer this question skillfully and with ease, your interviewer will trust in your capability as a worker.

115: What are the most difficult decisions for you to make?

Answer:

Explain your relationship to decision-making, and a general synopsis of the process you take in making choices. If there is a particular type of decision that you often struggle with, such as those that involve other people, make sure to explain why that type of decision is tough for you, and how you are currently engaged in improving your skills.

116: When making a tough decision, how do you gather information?

Answer:

If you're making a tough choice, it's best to gather information from as many sources as possible. Lead the interviewer through your process of taking information from people in different areas, starting first with advice from experts in your field, feedback from coworkers or other clients, and by looking analytically at your own past experiences.

117: Tell me about a decision you made that did not turn out well.

Answer:

Honesty and transparency are great values that your interviewer will appreciate - outline the choice you made, why you made it, the results of your poor decision - and finally (and most importantly!) what you learned from the decision. Give the interviewer reason to trust that you wouldn't make a decision like that again in the future.

118: Are you able to make decisions quickly?

Answer:

You may be able to make decisions quickly but be sure to communicate your skill in making sound, thorough decisions as well. Discuss the importance of making a decision quickly, and how you do so, as well as the necessity for each decision to first be well-informed.

Chapter 8

Goals

119: Ten years ago, what were your career goals?

Answer:

In reflecting back to what your career goals were ten years ago, it's important to show the ways in which you've made progress in that time. Draw distinct links between specific objectives that you've achieved and speak candidly about how it felt to reach those goals. Remain positive, upbeat, and growth-oriented, even if you haven't yet achieved all of the goals you set out to reach.

120: Tell me about a weakness you used to have, and how you changed it.

Answer:

Choose a non-professional weakness that you used to have and outline the process you went through in order to grow past it.

Explain the weakness itself, why it was problematic, the action steps you planned, how you achieved them, and the end result.

121: Tell me about your goal-setting process.

Answer:

When describing your goal-setting process, clearly outline the way that you create an outline for yourself. It may be helpful to offer an example of a particular goal you've set in the past and use this as a starting point to guide the way you created action steps, check-in points, and how the goal was eventually achieved.

122: Tell me about a time when you solved a problem by creating actionable steps to follow.

Answer:

This question will help the interviewer to see how you talented you are in outlining, problem resolution, and goal-setting. Explain thoroughly the procedure of outlining the problem, establishing steps to take, and then how you followed the steps (such as through check-in points along the way, or intermediary goals).

123: Where do you see yourself five years from now?

Answer:

Have some idea of where you would like to have advanced to in the position you're applying for, over the next several years. Make sure that your future plans line up with you still working for the company and stay positive about potential advancement. Focus on future opportunities, and what you're looking forward to - but make sure your reasons for advancement are admirable, such as greater experience and the chance to learn, rather than simply being out for a higher salary.

124: When in a position, do you look for opportunities to promote?

Answer:

There's a fine balance in this question - you want to show the interviewer that you have initiative and motivation to advance in your career, but not at the expense of appearing opportunistic or selfishly-motivated. Explain that you are always open to growth opportunities, and very willing to take on new responsibilities as your career advances.

125: On a scale of 1 to 10, how successful has your life been?

Answer:

Though you may still have a long list of goals to achieve, it's important to keep this answer positively-focused. Choose a high number between 7 and 9 and explain that you feel your life has been largely successful and satisfactory as a result of several specific achievements or experiences. Don't go as high as a 10, as the interviewer may not believe your response or in your ability to reason critically.

126: What is your greatest goal in life?

Answer:

It's okay for this answer to stray a bit into your personal life, but best if you can keep it professionally-focused. While specific goals are great, if your personal goal doesn't match up exactly with one of the company's objectives, you're better off keeping your goal a little more generic and encompassing, such as "success in my career" or "leading a happy and fulfilling life." Keep your answer brief, and show a decisive nature - most importantly, make it clear that you've already thought about this question and know what you want.

127: Tell me about a time when you set a goal in your personal life and achieved it.

Answer:

The interviewer can see that you excel at setting goals in your professional life, but he or she also wants to know that you are consistent in your life and capable of setting goals outside of the office as well. Use an example such as making a goal to eat more healthily or to drink more water and discuss what steps you outlined to achieve your goal, the process of taking action, and the final results as well.

128: What is your greatest goal in your career?

Answer:

Have a very specific goal of something you want to achieve in your career in mind and be sure that it's something the position clearly puts you in line to accomplish. Offer the goal as well as your plans to get there and emphasize clear ways in which this position will be an opportunity to work toward the goal.

129: Tell me about a time when you achieved a goal.

Answer:

Start out with how you set the goal, and why you chose it. Then, take the interviewer through the process of outlining the goal, taking steps to achieve it, the outcome, and finally, how you felt after achieving it or recognition you received. The most important part of this question includes the planning and implementation of strategies, so focus most of your time on explaining these aspects. However, the preliminary decisions and end results are also important, so make sure to include them as well.

130: What areas of your work would you still like to improve in? What are your plans to do this?

Answer:

While you may not want the interviewer to focus on things you could improve on, it's important to be self-aware of your own growth opportunities. More importantly, you can impress an interviewer by having specific goals and actions outlined in order to facilitate your growth, even if your area of improvement is something as simple as increasing sales or finding new ways to create greater efficiency.

This page is intentionally left blank

Chapter **9**

Creative Questions

131: Tell me about your favorite book or newspaper.

Answer:

The interviewer will look at your answer to this question in order to determine your ability to analyze and review critically. Additionally, try to choose something that is on a topic related to your field or that embodies a theme important to your work, and be able to explain how it relates. Stay away from controversial subject matter, such as politics or religion.

132: If you could be rich or famous, which would you choose?

Answer:

This question speaks to your ability to think creatively, but your answer may also give great insight to your character. If you answer rich, your interviewer may interpret that you are self-confident and don't seek approval from others, and that you like to be rewarded for your work. If you choose famous, your interviewer may gather that you like to be well-known and to deal with people, and to have the platform to deliver your message to others. Either way, it's important to back up your answer with sound reasoning.

133: If you could trade places with anyone for a week, who would it be and why?

Answer:

This question is largely designed to test your ability to think on your feet, and to come up with a reasonable answer to an outside the box question. Whoever you choose, explain your answer in a logical manner, and offer specific professional reasons that led you to choose the individual.

134: What would you say if I told you that just from glancing over your resume, I can already see three spelling mistakes?

Answer:

Clearly, your resume should be absolutely spotless - and you should be confident that it is. If your interviewer tries to make you second-guess yourself here, remain calm and poised and assert with a polite smile that you would be quite surprised as you are positive that your resume is error-free.

135: Tell me about your worldview.

Answer:

This question is designed to offer insight into your personality, so be aware of how the interviewer will interpret your answer. Speak openly and directly and try to incorporate your own job skills into your outlook on life. For example, discuss your beliefs on the ways that hard work and dedication can always bring success, or in how learning new things is one of life's greatest gifts. It's okay to expand into general life principles here but try to keep your thoughts related to the professional field as well.

136: What is the biggest mistake someone could make in an interview?

Answer:

The biggest mistake that could be made in an interview is to be caught off guard ! . Make sure that you don't commit whatever you answer here, and additionally be prepared for all questions. Other common mistakes include asking too early in the hiring process about job benefits, not having questions prepared when the interviewer asks if you have questions, arriving late, dressing casually or sloppily, or showing ignorance of the position.

137: If you won $50m lottery, what would you do with the money?

Answer:

While a question such as this may seem out of place in a job interview, it's important to display your creative thinking and your ability to think on the spot. It's also helpful if you choose something admirable, yet believable, to do with the money such as donate the first seventy percent to a charitable cause, and divide the remainder among gifts for friends, family, and of course, yourself.

138: Is there ever a time when honesty isn't appropriate in the workplace?

Answer:

This may be a difficult question, but the only time that honesty isn't appropriate in the workplace is perhaps when you're feeling anger or another emotion that is best kept to yourself. If this is the case, explain simply that it is best to put some thoughts aside, and clarify that the process of keeping some thoughts quiet is often enough to smooth over any unsettled emotions, thus eliminating the problem.

139: If you could travel anywhere in the world, where would it be?

Answer:

This question is meant to allow you to be creative - so go ahead and stretch your thoughts to come up with a unique answer. However, be sure to keep your answer professionally-minded. For example, choose somewhere rich with culture or that would expose you to a new experience, rather than going on an expensive cruise through the Bahamas.

140: What would I find in your refrigerator right now?

Answer:

An interviewer may ask a creative question such as this in order to discern your ability to answer unexpected questions calmly, or, to try to gain some insight into your personality. For example, candidates with a refrigerator full of junk food or take-out may be more likely to be under stress or have health issues, while a candidate with a balanced refrigerator full of nutritious staples may be more likely to lead a balanced mental life, as well.

141: If you could play any sport professionally, what would it be and what aspect draws you to it?

Answer:

Even if you don't know much about professional sports, this question might be a great opportunity to highlight some of your greatest professional working skills. For example, you may choose to play professional basketball, because you admire the teamwork and coordination that goes into creating a solid play. Or, you may choose to play professional tennis, because you consider yourself to be a go-getter with a solid work ethic and great dedication to perfecting your craft. Explain your choice simply to the interviewer without elaborating on drawn-out sports metaphors and be sure to point out specific areas or skills in which you excel.

142: Who were the presidential and vice-presidential candidates in the 2008 elections?

Answer:

This question, plain and simple, is intended as a gauge of your intelligence and awareness. If you miss this question, you may well fail the interview. Offer your response with a polite smile, because you understand that there are some individuals who probably miss this question.

143: Explain *X task* in a few short sentences as you would to a second-grader.

Answer:

An interviewer may ask you to break down a normal job task that you would complete in a manner that a child could understand, in part to test your knowledge of the task's inner workings - but in larger part, to test your ability to explain a process in simple, basic terms. While you and your coworkers may be able to converse using highly technical language, being able to simplify a process is an important skill for any employee to have.

144: If you could compare yourself to any animal, what would it be?

Answer:

Many interviewers ask this question, and it's not to determine which character traits you think you embody - instead, the interviewer wants to see that you can think outside the box, and that you're able to reason your way through any situation. Regardless of what animal you answer, be sure that you provide a thorough reason for your choice.

145: Who is your hero?

Answer:

Your hero may be your mother or father, an old professor, someone successful in your field, or perhaps even Wonder Woman - but keep your reasoning for your choice professional and be prepared to offer a logical train of thought. Choose someone who embodies values that are important in your chosen career field and answer the question with a smile and sense of passion.

146: Who would play you in the movie about your life?

Answer:

As with many creative questions that challenge an interviewee to think outside the box, the answer to this question is not as important as how you answer it. Choose a professional, and relatively non-controversial actor or actress, and then be prepared to offer specific reasoning for your choice, employing important skills or traits you possess.

147: Name five people, alive or dead, that would be at your ideal dinner party?

Answer:

Smile and sound excited at the opportunity to think outside the box when asked this question, even if it seems to come from left field. Choose dynamic, inspiring individuals who you could truly learn from, and explain what each of them would have to offer to the conversation. Don't forget to include yourself, and to talk about what you would bring to the conversation as well!

This page is intentionally left blank

Chapter **10**

Customer Service

148: What is customer service?

Answer:

Customer service can be many things - and the most important consideration in this question is that you have a creative answer. Demonstrate your ability to think outside the box by offering a confident answer that goes past a basic definition, and that shows you have truly considered your own individual view of what it means to take care of your customers. The thoughtful consideration you hold for customers will speak for itself.

149: Tell me about a time when you went out of your way for a customer.

Answer:

It's important that you offer an example of a time you truly went out of your way - be careful not to confuse something that felt like a big effort on your part, with something your employer would expect you to do anyway. Offer an example of the customer's problems, what you did to solve it, and the way the customer responded after you took care of the situation.

150: How do you gain confidence from customers?

Answer:

This is a very open-ended question that allows you to show your customer service skills to the interviewer. There are many possible answers, and it is best to choose something that you've had great experience with, such as "by handling situations with transparency," "offering rewards," or "focusing on great communication." Offer specific examples of successes you've had.

151: Tell me about a time when a customer was upset or agitated - how did you handle the situation?

Answer:

Similarly, to handling a dispute with another employee, the most important part to answering this question is to first set up the scenario, offer a step-by-step guide to your particular conflict resolution style, and end by describing the way the conflict was resolved. Be sure that in answering questions about your own conflict resolution style, that you emphasize the importance of open communication and understanding from both parties, as well as a willingness to reach a compromise or other solution.

152: When can you make an exception for a customer?

Answer:

Exceptions for customers can generally be made when in accordance with company policy or when directed by a supervisor. Display an understanding of the types of situations in which an exception should be considered, such as when a customer has endured a particular hardship, had a complication with an order, or at a request.

153: What would you do in a situation where you were needed by both a customer and your boss?

Answer:

While both your customer and your boss have different needs of you and are very important to your success as a worker, it is always best to try to attend to your customer first - however, the key is explaining to your boss why you are needed urgently by the customer, and then to assure your boss that you will attend to his or her needs as soon as possible (unless it's absolutely an urgent matter).

154: What is the most important aspect of customer service?

Answer:

While many people would simply state that customer satisfaction is the most important aspect of customer service, it's important to be able to elaborate on other important techniques in customer service situations. Explain why customer service is such a key part of business and be sure to expand on the aspect that you deem to be the most important in a way that is reasoned and well-thought out.

155: Is it best to create low or high expectations for a customer?

Answer:

You may answer this question either way (after, of course, determining that the company does not have a clear opinion on the matter). However, no matter which way you answer the question, you must display a thorough thought process, and very clear reasoning for the option you chose. Offer pros and cons of each and include the ultimate point that tips the scale in favor of your chosen answer.

Chapter **11**

Background and Experience

156: Why did you choose your college major?

Answer:

It's important to display interest in your work, and if your major is related to your current field, it will be simple for you to relate the two. Perhaps you even knew while in college that you wanted to do a job similar to this position, and so you chose the major so as to receive the education and training you needed to succeed. If your major doesn't relate clearly, it's still important to express a sense of passion for your choice, and to specify the importance of pursuing something that matters to you - which is how you made the decision to come to your current career field instead.

157: Tell me about your college experience.

Answer:

It's best to keep this answer positive - don't focus on parties, pizza, or procrastinating. Instead, offer a general summary of the benefits you received in college, followed by an anecdote of a favorite professor or course that opened up your way of thinking about the field you're in. This is a great opportunity for you to show your passion for your career, make sure to answer enthusiastically and confidently.

158: What is the most unique thing about yourself that you would bring to this position?

Answer:

This question is often asked as a close to an interview, and it gives you a final chance to highlight your best qualities to the employer. Treat the question like a sort of review, and explain why your specific mix of education, experience, and passions will be the ideal combination for the employer. Remain confident but humble and keep your answer to about two minutes.

159: How did your last job stand up to your previous expectations of it?

Answer:

While it's okay to discuss what you learned if you expected too much out of a previous job, it's best to keep this question away from negative statements or portrayals. Focus your answer around what your previous job did hold that you had expected, and how much you enjoyed those aspects of the position.

160: How did you become interested in this field?

Answer:

This is the chance for you to show your passion for your career - and the interviewer will be assured that you are a great candidate if it's obvious that you enjoy your job. You can include a brief anecdote here in order to make your interest personal but be sure that it is brief. Offer specific names of mentors or professors who aided in your discovery and make it clear that you love what you do.

161: What was the greatest thing you learned while in school?

Answer:

By offering a lesson you learned outside of the classroom, you can show the interviewer your capacity for creativity, learning, and reflection. The practical lessons you learned in the classroom are certainly invaluable in their own right and may pertain closely to the position but showing the mastery of a concept that you had to learn on your own will highlight your growth potential.

162: Tell me about a time when you had to learn a different skill set for a new position.

Answer:

Use a specific example to describe what you had to learn and how you set about outlining goals and tasks for yourself. It's important to show that you mastered the skill largely from your dedication to learning it, and because of the systematic approach you took to developing and honing your individual education. Additionally, draw connections between the skill you learned and the new position, and show how well prepared you are for the job.

163: Tell me about a person who has been a great influence in your career.

Answer:

It's important to make this answer easy to relate to - your story should remind the interviewer of the person who was most influential in his or her own career. Explain what you learned from this person and why they inspired you, and how you hope to model them later in your career with future successes.

164: What would this person tell me about you?

Answer:

Most importantly, if this person is one of your references - they had better know who you are! There are all too many horror stories of professors or past employers being called for a reference, and not being able to recall when they knew you or why you were remarkable, which doesn't send a very positive message to potential employers. This person should remember you as being enthusiastic, passionate, and motivated to learn and succeed.

165: What is the most productive time of day for you?

Answer:

This is a trick question - you should be equally productive all day! While it's normal to become extra motivated for certain projects, and also true that some tasks will require additional work, be sure to emphasize to the interviewer that working diligently throughout the entirety of the day comes naturally to you.

166: What was the most responsibility you were given at your previous job?

Answer:

This question provides you with an opportunity to elaborate on responsibilities that may or may not be on your resume. For instance, your resume may not have allowed room to discuss individual projects you worked on that were really outside the scope of your job responsibilities, but you can tell the interviewer here about the additional work you did and how it translated into new skills and a richer career experience for you.

167: Do you believe you were compensated fairly at your last job?

Answer:

Remember to stay positive, and to avoid making negative comments about your previous employer. If you were not compensated fairly, simply state that you believe your qualities and experience were outside the compensation limitations of the old job, and that you're looking forward to an opportunity that is more in line with the place you're at in your career.

168: Tell me about a time when you received feedback on your work and enacted it.

Answer:

Try to give an example of feedback your received early in your career, and the steps you took to incorporate it with your work. The most important part of this question is to display the way you learned from the feedback, as well as your willingness to accept suggestions from your superiors. Be sure to offer reflection and understanding of how the feedback helped your work to improve.

169: Tell me about a time when you received feedback on your work that you did not agree with, or thought was unfair. How did you handle it?

Answer:

When explaining that you did not agree with particular feedback or felt it was unfair, you'll need to justify tactfully why the feedback was inaccurate. Then, explain how you communicated directly with the person who offered the feedback, and, most importantly, how you listened to their response, analyzed it, and then came to a mutual agreement.

170: What was your favorite job, and why?

Answer:

It's best if your favorite job relates to the position you're currently applying for, as you can then easily draw connections between why you enjoyed that job and why you are interested in the current position. Additionally, it is extremely important to explain why you've qualified the particular job as your favorite, and what aspects of it you would look for in another job, so that the interviewer can determine whether or not you are a good fit.

171: Tell me about an opportunity that your last position did not allow you to achieve.

Answer:

Stay focused on the positive and be understanding of the limitations of your previous position. Give a specific example of a goal or career objective that you were not able to achieve, but rather than expressing disappointment over the missed opportunity, discuss the ways you're looking forward to the chance to grow in a new position.

172: Tell me about the worst boss you ever had.

Answer:

It's important to keep this answer brief, and positively focused. While you may offer a couple of short, critical assessments of your boss, focus on the things you learned from working with such an individual, and remain sympathetic to challenges the boss may have faced.

This page is intentionally left blank

Chapter **12**

Business Skills and Knowledge

173: What is the best way for a company to advertise?

Answer:

If you're going for a position in any career other than marketing, this question is probably intended to demonstrate your ability to think critically and to provide reflective support for your answers. As such, the particular method you choose is not so important as why you've chosen it. For example, word of mouth advertising is important because customers will inherently trust the source, and social media advertising is important as it reaches new customers quickly and cheaply.

174: Is it better to gain a new customer or to keep an old one?

Answer:

In almost every case, it is better to keep an old customer, and it's important that you are able to articulate why this is. First, new customers generally cost companies more than retaining old ones does, and new customers are more likely to switch to a different company. Additionally, keeping old customers is a great way to provide a stable backbone for the company, as well as to also gain new customers as they are likely to recommend your company to friends.

175: What is the best way to win clients from competitors?

Answer:

There are many schools of thought on the best way to win clients from competitors, and unless you know that your interviewer adheres to a specific thought or practice, it's best to keep this question general. Rather than using absolute language, focus on the benefits of one or two strategies and show a clear, critical understanding of how these ways can succeed in a practical application.

176: How do you feel about companies monitoring internet usage?

Answer:

Generally speaking, most companies will monitor some degree of internet usage over their employees - and during an interview is not the best time to rebel against this practice. Instead, focus on positive aspects such as the way it can lead to increased productivity for some employees who may be easily lost in the world of resourceful information available to them.

177: What is your first impression of our company?

Answer:

Obviously, this should be a positive answer! Pick out a couple key components of the company's message or goals that you especially identify with or that pertain to your experience and discuss why you believe these missions are so important.

178: Tell me about your personal philosophy on business.

Answer:

Your personal philosophy on business should be well-thought out, and in line with the missions and objectives of the company. Stay focused on positive aspects such as the service it can provide, and the lessons people gain in business, and offer insight as to where your philosophy has come from.

179: What's most important in a business model: sales, customer service, marketing, management, etc.?

Answer:

For many positions, it may be a good strategy to tailor this answer to the type of field you're working in, and to explain why that aspect of business is key. However, by explaining that each aspect is integral to the function as a whole, you can display a greater sense of business savvy to the interviewer and may stand out in his or her mind as a particularly aware candidate.

180: How do you keep up with news and emerging trends in the field?

Answer:

The interviewer wants to see that you are aware of what's currently going on in your field. It is important that your education does not stop after college, and the most successful candidates will have a list of resources they regularly turn to already in place, so that they may stay aware and engaged in developing trends.

181: Would you have a problem adhering to company policies on social media?

Answer:

Social media concerns in the workplace have become a greater issue, and many companies now outline policies for the use of social media. Interviewers will want to be assured that you won't have a problem adhering to company standards, and that you will maintain a consistent, professional image both in the office and online.

182: Tell me about one of the greatest problems facing *X industry* today.

Answer:

If you're involved in your career field and spend time on your own studying trends and new developments, you should be able to display an awareness of both problems and potential solutions coming up in the industry. Research some of the latest news before heading into the interview and be prepared to discuss current events thoroughly.

183: What do you think it takes to be successful in our company?

Answer:

Research the company prior to the interview. Be aware of the company's mission and main objectives, as well as some of the biggest names in the company, and also keep in mind how they achieved success. Keep your answer focused on specific objectives you could reach in order to help the company achieve its goals.

184: What is your favorite part of working in this career field?

Answer:

This question is an opportunity to discuss some of your favorite aspects of the job, and to highlight why you are a great candidate for the particular position. Choose elements of the work you enjoy that are related to what you would do if hired for the position. Remember to remain enthusiastic and excited for the opportunities you could attain in the job.

185: What do you see happening to your career in the next 10 years?

Answer:

If you're plugged in to what's happening in your career now and are making an effort to stay abreast of emerging trends in your field, you should be able to offer the interviewer several predictions as to where your career or field may be heading. This insight and level of awareness shows a level of dedication and interest that is important to employers.

This page is intentionally left blank

Chapter **13**

Communication

186: Describe a time when you communicated a difficult or complicated idea to a co-worker.

Answer:

Start by explaining the idea briefly to the interviewer, and then give an overview of why it was necessary to break it down further to the coworker. Finally, explain the idea in succinct steps, so the interviewer can see your communication abilities and skill in simplification.

187: What situations do you find it difficult to communicate in?

Answer:

Even great communicators will often find particular situations that are more difficult to communicate effectively in, so don't be afraid to answer this question honestly. Be sure to explain why the particular situation you name is difficult for you and try to choose an uncommon answer such as language barrier or in time of hardship, rather than a situation such as speaking to someone of higher authority.

188: What are the key components of good communication?

Answer:

Some of the components of good communication include an environment that is free from distractions, feedback from the listener, and revision or clarification from the speaker when necessary. Refer to basic communication models where necessary and offer to go through a role-play sample with the interviewer in order to show your skills.

189: Tell me about a time when you solved a problem through communication.

Answer:

Solving problems through communication is key in the business world, so choose a specific situation from your previous job in which you navigated a messy situation by communicating effectively through the conflict. Explain the basis of the situation, as well as the communication steps you took, and end with a discussion of why communicating through the problem was so important to its resolution.

190: Tell me about a time when you had a dispute with another employee. How did you resolve the situation?

Answer:

Make sure to use a specific instance, and explain step-by-step the scenario, what you did to handle it, and how it was finally resolved. The middle step, how you handled the dispute, is clearly the most definitive - describe the types of communication you used, and how you used compromise to reach a decision. Conflict resolution is an important skill for any employee to have and is one that interviewers will search for to determine both how likely you are to be involved in disputes, and how likely they are to be forced to become involved in the dispute if one arises.

191: Do you build relationships quickly with people, or take more time to get to know them?

Answer:

Either of these options can display good qualities, so determine which style is more applicable to you. Emphasize the steps you take in relationship-building over the particular style and summarize briefly why this works best for you.

192: Describe a time when you had to work through office politics to solve a problem.

Answer:

Try to focus on the positives in this question, so that you can use the situation to your advantage. Don't portray your previous employer negatively, and instead use a minimal instance (such as paperwork or a single individual), to highlight how you worked through a specific instance resourcefully. Give examples of communication skills or problem-solving you used in order to achieve a resolution.

193: Tell me about a time when you persuaded others to take on a difficult task.

Answer:

This question is an opportunity to highlight both your leadership and communication skills. While the specific situation itself is important to offer as background, focus on how you were able to persuade the others, and what tactics worked the best.

194: Tell me about a time when you successfully persuaded a group to accept your proposal.

Answer:

This question is designed to determine your resourcefulness and your communication skills. Explain the ways in which you took into account different perspectives within the group and created a presentation that would be appealing and convincing to all members. Additionally, you can pump up the proposal itself by offering details about it that show how well-executed it was.

195: Tell me about a time when you had a problem with another person, that, in hindsight, you wished you had handled differently.

Answer:

The key to this question is to show your capabilities of reflection and your learning process. Explain the situation, how you handled it at the time, what the outcome of the situation was, and finally, how you would handle it now. Most importantly, tell the interviewer why you would handle it differently now - did your previous solution create stress on the relationship with the other person, or do you wish that you had stood up more for what you wanted? While you shouldn't elaborate on how poorly you handled the situation before, the most important thing is to show that you've grown and reached a deeper level of understanding as a result of the conflict.

196: Tell me about a time when you negotiated a conflict between other employees.

Answer:

An especially important question for those interviewing for a supervisory role - begin with a specific situation and explain how you communicated effectively to each individual. For example, did you introduce a compromise? Did you make an executive decision? Or, did you perform as a mediator and encourage the employees to reach a conclusion on their own?

This page is intentionally left blank

Chapter **14**

Job Searching and Scheduling

197: What are the three most important things you're looking for in a position?

Answer:

The top three things you want in a position should be similar to the top three things the employer wants from an employee, so that it is clear that you are well-matched to the job. For example, the employer wants a candidate who is well-qualified for and has practical experience - and you want a position that allows you to use your education and skills to their best applications. The employer wants a candidate who is willing to take on new challenges and develop new systems to increase sales or productivity - and you want a position that pushes you and offers opportunities to develop, create, and lead new initiatives. The employer wants a candidate who will grow into and stay with the company for a long time - and you want a position that offers stability and believes in building a strong team. Research what the employer is looking for beforehand and match your objectives to theirs.

198: How are you evaluating the companies you're looking to work with?

Answer:

While you may feel uncomfortable exerting your own requirements during the interview, the employer wants to see that you are thinking critically about the companies you're applying with, just as they are critically looking at you. Don't be afraid to specify what your needs from a company are (but do try to make sure they match up well with the company - preferably before you apply there) and show confidence and decisiveness in your answer. The interviewer wants to know that you're the kind of person who knows what they want, and how to get it.

199: Are you comfortable working for _____ salary?

Answer:

If the answer to this question is no, it may be a bit of a deal-breaker in a first interview, as you are unlikely to have much room to negotiate. You can try to leverage a bit by highlighting specific experience you have, and how that makes you qualified for more, but be aware that this is very difficult to navigate at this step of the process. To avoid this situation, be aware of industry standards and, if possible, company standards, prior to your application.

200: Why did you choose your last job?

Answer:

In learning what led you to your last job, the interviewer is able to get a feel for the types of things that motivate you. Keep these professionally-focused and remain passionate about the early points of your career, and how excited you were to get started in the field.

201: How long has it been since your last job and why?

Answer:

Be sure to have an explanation prepared for all gaps in employment, and make sure it's a professional reason. Don't mention difficulties you may have had in finding a job, and instead focus on positive things such as pursuing outside interests or perhaps returning to school for additional education.

202: What other types of jobs have you been looking for?

Answer:

The answer to this question can show the interviewer that you're both on the market and in demand. Mention jobs you've applied for or looked at that are closely related to your field, or similar to the position you're interviewing for. Don't bring up last-ditch efforts that found you applying for a part-time job completely unrelated to your field.

203: Have you ever been disciplined at work?

Answer:

Hopefully the answer here is no - but if you have been disciplined for something at work though, be absolutely sure that you can explain it thoroughly. Detail what you learned from the situation and reflect on how you grew after the process.

204: What is your availability like?

Answer:

Your availability should obviously be as open as possible, and any gaps in availability should be explained and accounted for. Avoid asking about vacation or personal days (as well as other benefits) and convey to the interviewer how serious you are about your work.

205: May I contact your current employer?

Answer:

If possible, it is best to allow an interviewer to contact your current employer as a reference. However, if it's important that your employer is not contacted, explain your reason tactfully, such as you just started job searching and you haven't had the opportunity yet to inform them that you are looking for other employment. Be careful of this reasoning though, as employers may wonder if you'll start shopping for something better while employed with them as well.

206: Do you have any valuable contacts you could bring to our business?

Answer:

It's great if you can bring knowledge, references, or other contacts that your new employer may be able to network with. However, be sure that you aren't offering up any of your previous employer's clients, or in any way violating contractual agreements.

207: How soon would you be available to start working?

Answer:

While you want to be sure that you're available to start as soon as possible if the company is interested in hiring you, if you still have another job, be sure to give them at least two weeks' notice. Though your new employer may be anxious for you to start, they will want to hire a worker whom they can respect for giving adequate notice, so that they won't have to worry if you'll eventually leave them in the lurch.

208: Why would your last employer say that you left?

Answer:

The key to this question is that your employer's answer must be the same as your own answer about why you left. For instance, if you've told your employer that you left to find a position with greater opportunities for career advancement, your employer had better not say that you were let go for missing too many days of work. Honesty is key in your job application process.

209: How long have you been actively looking for a job?

Answer:

It's best if you haven't been actively looking for a job for very long, as a long period of time may make the interviewer wonder why no one else has hired you. If it has been awhile, make sure to explain why, and keep it positive. Perhaps you haven't come across many opportunities that provide you with enough of a challenge or that are adequately matched to someone of your education and experience.

210: When don't you show up to work?

Answer:

Clearly, the only time acceptable to miss work is for a real emergency or when you're truly sick - so don't start bringing up times now that you plan to miss work due to vacations or family birthdays. Alternatively, you can tell the interviewer how dedicated to your work you are, and how you always strive to be fully present and to put in the same amount of work every time you come in, even when you're feeling slightly under the weather.

211: What is the most common reason you miss work?

Answer:

If there is a reason that you will miss work routinely, this is the time to disclose it - but doing so during an interview will reflect negatively on you. Ideally, you will only miss work during cases of extreme illness or other emergencies.

212: What is your attendance record like?

Answer:

Be sure to answer this question honestly, but ideally you will have already put in the work to back up the fact that you rarely miss days or arrive late. However, if there are gaps in your attendance, explain them briefly with appropriate reasons, and make sure to emphasize your dedication to your work, and reliability.

213: Where did you hear about this position?

Answer:

This may seem like a simple question, but the answer can actually speak volumes about you. If you were referred by a friend or another employee who works for the company, this is a great chance to mention your connection (if the person is in good standing!). However, if you heard about it from somewhere like a career fair or a work placement agency, you may want to focus on how pleased you were to come across such a wonderful opportunity.

214: Tell me anything else you'd like me to know when making a hiring decision.

Answer:

This is a great opportunity for you to give a final sell of yourself to the interviewer - use this time to remind the interviewer of why you are qualified for the position, and what you can bring to the company that no one else can. Express your excitement for the opportunity to work with a company pursuing X *mission*.

This page is intentionally left blank

Chapter **15**

Knowledge of the Company

215: Why would your skills be a good match with *X objective* **of our company?**

Answer:

If you've researched the company before the interview, answering this question should be no problem. Determine several of the company's main objectives and explain how specific skills that you have are conducive to them. Also, think about ways that your experience and skills can translate to helping the company expand upon these objectives, and to reach further goals. If your old company had a similar objective, give a specific example of how you helped the company to meet it.

216: What do you think this job entails?

Answer:

Make sure you've researched the position well before heading into the interview. Read any and all job descriptions you can find (at best, directly from the employer's website or job posting), and make note of key duties, responsibilities, and experience required. Few things are less impressive to an interviewer than a candidate who has no idea what sort of job they're actually being interviewed for.

217: Is there anything else about the job or company you'd like to know?

Answer:

If you have learned about the company beforehand, this is a great opportunity to show that you put in the effort to study before the interview. Ask questions about the company's mission in relation to current industry trends, and engage the interviewer in interesting, relevant conversation. Additionally, clear up anything else you need to know about the specific position before leaving - so that if the interviewer calls with an offer, you'll be prepared to answer.

218: Are you the best candidate for this position?

Answer:

Yes! Offer specific details about what makes you qualified for this position and be sure to discuss (and show) your unbridled passion and enthusiasm for the new opportunity, the job, and the company.

219: How did you prepare for this interview?

Answer:

The key part of this question is to make sure that you have prepared! Be sure that you've researched the company, their objectives, and their services prior to the interview, and know as much about the specific position as you possibly can. It's also helpful to learn about the company's history and key players in the current organization.

220: If you were hired here, what would you do on your first day?

Answer:

While many people will answer this question in a boring fashion, going through the standard first day procedures, this question is actually a great chance for you to show the interviewer why you will make a great hire. In addition to things like going through training or orientation, emphasize how much you would enjoy meeting your supervisors and coworkers, or how you would spend a lot of the day asking questions and taking in all of your new surroundings.

221: Have you viewed our company's website?

Answer:

Clearly, you should have viewed the company's website and done some preliminary research on them before coming to the interview. If for some reason you did not, do not say that you did, as the interviewer may reveal you by asking a specific question about it. If you did look at the company's website, this is an appropriate time to bring up something you saw there that was of particular interest to you, or a value that you especially supported.

222: How does X experience on your resume relate to this position?

Answer:

Many applicants will have some bit of experience on their resume that does not clearly translate to the specific job in question. However, be prepared to be asked about this type of seemingly-irrelevant experience, and have a response prepared that takes into account similar skill sets or training that the two may share.

223: Why do you want this position?

Answer:

Keep this answer focused positively on aspects of this specific job that will allow you to further your skills, offer new experience, or that will be an opportunity for you to do something that you particularly enjoy. Don't tell the interviewer that you've been looking for a job for a long time, or that the pay is very appealing, or you will appear unmotivated and opportunistic.

224: How is your background relevant to this position?

Answer:

Ideally, this should be obvious from your resume. However, in instances where your experience is more loosely-related to the position, make sure that you've researched the job and company well before the interview. That way, you can intelligently relate the experience and skills that you do have, to similar skills that would be needed in the new position. Explain specifically how your skills will translate and use words to describe your background such as "preparation" and "learning." Your prospective position should be described as an "opportunity" and a chance for "growth and development."

225: How do you feel about X *mission* of our company?

Answer:

It's important to have researched the company prior to the interview - and if you've done so, this question won't catch you off guard. The best answer is one that is simple, to the point, and shows knowledge of the mission at hand. Offer a few short statements as to why you believe in the mission's importance and note that you would be interested in the chance to work with a company that supports it.

INDEX

HR Interview Questions

Creativity

1:   Every business faces problems that affect productivity and profitability. Can you share with me a solution you developed for a workplace problem that was unusual or unexpected, and actually led to increased productivity or profitability?

2:   Can you describe how you analyzed a workplace problem you have faced, and how your analysis led to the solution?

3:   There are times when customers are unhappy with your company's product or service and expect a solution that is more than what is normally provided. Can you share a time when you were able to provide a solution to an unusual customer expectation that made both customer and management happy?

4:   Describe workplace innovations you have developed on your own initiative.

5:   Describe workplace innovations you helped developed as a member of a team.

6:   Where do you find ideas?

7:   How do you achieve creativity in the workplace?

8:   How do you push others to create ideas?

9:   Describe your creativity.

Leadership

10:   Was there a time you were called upon to reorganize your department? If so, what steps did you take to ensure the reorganization was successful?

11:   Tell me about a time when you led a team to successfully complete a project.

12:   Describe a time when you played a major leadership role in a special event.

13: How have the people around you responded to your leadership efforts?

14: Describe your strengths as a leader.

15: Describe the greatest weakness in your leadership style.

16: If a group of people in your department were talking about you behind your back, what do you think they would be saying about you?

17: Describe a difficult project that required you to build consensus on a divisive issue.

18: Describe a project or task that required you to develop agreement or cooperation between departments.

19: Describe a situation when you needed to build support within your department for an idea you thought would greatly benefit your company.

20: Would you rather receive more authority or more responsibility at work?

21: What do you do when someone in a group isn't contributing their fair share?

22: Tell me about a time when you made a decision that was outside of your authority.

23: Are you comfortable going to supervisors with disputes?

24: If you had been in charge at your last job, what would you have done differently?

25: Do you believe employers should praise or reward employees for a job well done?

26: What do you believe is the most important quality a leader can have?

27: Tell me about a time when an unforeseen problem arose. How did you handle it?

28: Can you give me an example of a time when you were able to improve X *objective* at your previous job?

29: Tell me about a time when a supervisor did not provide specific enough direction on a project.

30: Tell me about a time when you were in charge of leading a project.

31:   Tell me about a suggestion you made to a former employer that was later implemented.

32:   Tell me about a time when you thought of a way something in the workplace could be done more efficiently.

33:   Is there a difference between leading and managing people - which is your greater strength?

34:   Do you function better in a leadership role, or as a worker on a team?

35:   Tell me about a time when you discovered something in the workplace that was disrupting your (or others) productivity - what did you do about it.

36:   How do you perform in a job with clearly-defined objectives and goals?

37:   How do you perform in a job where you have great decision-making power?

38:   If you saw another employee doing something dishonest or unethical, what would you do?

39:   Tell me about a time when you learned something on your own that later helped in your professional life.

40:   Tell me about a time when you developed a project idea at work.

41:   Tell me about a time when you took a risk on a project.

42:   What would you tell someone who was looking to get into this field?

Teamwork

43:   How would you handle a negative coworker?

44:   What would you do if you witnessed a coworker surfing the web, reading a book, etc, wasting company time?

45:   How do you handle competition among yourself and other employees?

46:   When is it okay to socialize with coworkers?

47:   Tell me about a time when a major change was made at your last job, and how you handled it.

48:   When delegating tasks, how do you choose which tasks go to which team members?

49: Tell me about a time when you had to stand up for something you believed strongly about to coworkers or a supervisor.

50: Tell me about a time when you helped someone finish their work, even though it wasn't "your job."

51: What are the challenges of working on a team? How do you handle this?

52: Do you value diversity in the workplace?

53: How would you handle a situation in which a coworker was not accepting of someone else's diversity?

54: Are you rewarded more from working on a team, or accomplishing a task on your own?

Deadlines and Time Management

55: Tell me about a time when you didn't meet a deadline.

56: How do you eliminate distractions while working?

57: Tell me about a time when you worked in a position with a weekly or monthly quota to meet. How often were you successful?

58: Tell me about a time when you met a tough deadline, and how you were able to complete it.

59: How do you stay organized when you have multiple projects on your plate?

60: How much time during your work day do you spend on "auto-pilot?"

61: How do you handle deadlines?

62: Tell me about your personal problem-solving process.

63: What sort of things at work can make you stressed?

64: What do you look like when you are stressed about something? How do you solve it?

65: Can you multi-task?

66: How many hours per week do you work?

67: How many times per day do you check your email?

Dedication and Attitude

68: Tell me about a time when you worked additional hours to finish a project.

69: Tell me about a time when your performance exceeded the duties and requirements of your job.

70: What is your driving attitude about work?

71: Do you take work home with you?

72: Describe a typical work day to me.

73: Tell me about a time when you went out of your way at your previous job.

74: Are you open to receiving feedback and criticisms on your job performance, and adjusting as necessary?

75: What inspires you?

76: How do you inspire others?

Personality

77: What has been your biggest success?

78: What motivates you?

79: What do you do when you lose motivation?

80: What do you like to do in your free time?

81: What sets you apart from other workers?

82: Why are you the best candidate for that position?

83: What does it take to be successful?

84: What would be the biggest challenge in this position for you?

85: Would you describe yourself as an introvert or an extrovert?

86: What are some positive character traits that you don't possess?

87: What is the greatest lesson you've ever learned?

88: Have you ever been in a situation where one of your strengths became a weakness in an alternate setting?

89: Who has been the most influential person in your life?

90: Do you consider yourself to be a "detailed" or "big picture" type of person?

91: What is your greatest fear?

92: What sort of challenges do you enjoy?

93: Tell me about a time you were embarrassed. How did you handle it?

94: What is your greatest weakness?

95: What are the three best adjectives to describe you in a work setting?

96: What are the three best adjectives to describe you in your personal life?

97: What type of worker are you?

98: Tell me about your happiest day at work.

99: Tell me about your worst day at work.

100: What are you passionate about?

101: What is the piece of criticism you receive most often?

102: What type of work environment do you succeed the most in?

103: Are you an emotional person?

Decision Making

104: Have you come across any decision-making situations in the past?

105: How will you make decisions under pressure?

106: Do you think it is always important to make ethically correct decisions?

107: Does your emotional maturity play a role in making decisions?

108: According to you, decision-making should be done by the manager or by a team?

109: Good business decisions are based on sound empirical evidence. Do you agree with this view?

110: When do you think a team can be involved in decision-making?

111: Do you think decision-making is a form of planning? If yes, what is the similarity between the two?

112: In a financial services company like ours how do you think decisions should be made?

113: What are the steps to be followed in attaining a decision?

114: How do you make decisions?

115: What are the most difficult decisions for you to make?

116: When making a tough decision, how do you gather information?

117: Tell me about a decision you made that did not turn out well.

118: Are you able to make decisions quickly?

Goals

119: Ten years ago, what were your career goals?

120: Tell me about a weakness you used to have, and how you changed it.

121: Tell me about your goal-setting process.

122: Tell me about a time when you solved a problem by creating actionable steps to follow.

123: Where do you see yourself five years from now?

124: When in a position, do you look for opportunities to promote?

125: On a scale of 1 to 10, how successful has your life been?

126: What is your greatest goal in life?

127: Tell me about a time when you set a goal in your personal life and achieved it.

128: What is your greatest goal in your career?

129: Tell me about a time when you achieved a goal.

130: What areas of your work would you still like to improve in? What are your plans to do this?

Creative Questions

131: Tell me about your favorite book or newspaper.

132: If you could be rich or famous, which would you choose?

133: If you could trade places with anyone for a week, who would it be and why?

134: What would you say if I told you that just from glancing over your resume I can already see three spelling mistakes?

135: Tell me about your worldview.

136: What is the biggest mistake someone could make in an interview?

137: If you won the $50m lottery, what would you do with the money?

138: Is there ever a time when honesty isn't appropriate in the workplace?

139: If you could travel anywhere in the world, where would it be?

140: What would I find in your refrigerator right now?

141: If you could play any sport professionally, what would it be and what aspect draws you to it?

142: Who were the presidential and vice-presidential candidates in the 2008 elections?

143: Explain X *task* in a few short sentences as you would to a second-grader.

144: If you could compare yourself to any animal, what would it be?

145: Who is your hero?

146: Who would play you in the movie about your life?

147: Name five people, alive or dead, that would be at your ideal dinner party?

Customer Service

148: What is customer service?

149: Tell me about a time when you went out of your way for a customer.

150: How do you gain confidence from customers?

151: Tell me about a time when a customer was upset or agitated - how did you handle the situation.

152: When can you make an exception for a customer?

153: What would you do in a situation where you were needed by both a customer and your boss?

154: What is the most important aspect of customer service?

155: Is it best to create low or high expectations for a customer?

Background and Experience

156: Why did you choose your college major?

157: Tell me about your college experience.

158: What is the most unique thing about yourself that you would bring to this position?

159: How did your last job stand up to your previous expectations of it?

160: How did you become interested in this field?

161: What was the greatest thing you learned while in school?

162: Tell me about a time when you had to learn a different skill set for a new position.

163: Tell me about a person who has been a great influence in your career.

164: What would this person tell me about you?

165: What is the most productive time of day for you?

166: What was the most responsibility you were given at your previous job?

167: Do you believe you were compensated fairly at your last job?

168: Tell me about a time when you received feedback on your work, and enacted it.

169: Tell me about a time when you received feedback on your work that you did not agree with, or thought was unfair. How did you handle it?

170: What was your favorite job, and why?

171: Tell me about an opportunity that your last position did not allow you to achieve.

172: Tell me about the worst boss you ever had.

Business Skills and Knowledge

173: What is the best way for a company to advertise?

174: Is it better to gain a new customer or to keep an old one?

175: What is the best way to win clients from competitors?

176: How do you feel about companies monitoring internet usage?

177: What is your first impression of our company?

178: Tell me about your personal philosophy on business.

179: What's most important in a business model: sales, customer service, marketing, management, etc.?

180: How do you keep up with news and emerging trends in the field?

181: Would you have a problem adhering to company policies on social media?

182: Tell me about one of the greatest problems facing *X industry* today.

183: What do you think it takes to be successful in our company?

184: What is your favorite part of working in this career field?

185: What do you see happening to your career in the next 10 years?

Communication

186: Describe a time when you communicated a difficult or complicated idea to a co-worker.

187: What situations do you find it difficult to communicate in?

188: What are the key components of good communication?

189: Tell me about a time when you solved a problem through communication.

190: Tell me about a time when you had a dispute with another employee. How did you resolve the situation?

191: Do you build relationships quickly with people, or take more time to get to know them?

192: Describe a time when you had to work through office politics to solve a problem.

193: Tell me about a time when you persuaded others to take on a difficult task.

194: Tell me about a time when you successfully persuaded a group to accept your proposal.

195: Tell me about a time when you had a problem with another person, that, in hindsight, you wished you had handled differently.

196: Tell me about a time when you negotiated a conflict between other employees.

Job Searching and Scheduling

197: What are the three most important things you're looking for in a position?

198: How are you evaluating the companies you're looking to work with?

199: Are you comfortable working for _____ salary?

200: Why did you choose your last job?

201: How long has it been since your last job and why?

202: What other types of jobs have you been looking for?

203: Have you ever been disciplined at work?

204: What is your availability like?

205: May I contact your current employer?

206: Do you have any valuable contacts you could bring to our business?

207: How soon would you be available to start working?

208: Why would your last employer say that you left?

209: How long have you been actively looking for a job?

210: When don't you show up to work?

211: What is the most common reason you miss work?

212: What is your attendance record like?

213: Where did you hear about this position?

214: Tell me anything else you'd like me to know when making a hiring decision.

Knowledge of the Company

215: Why would your skills be a good match with X objective of our company?

216: What do you think this job entails?

217: Is there anything else about the job or company you'd like to know?

218: Are you the best candidate for this position?

219: How did you prepare for this interview?

220: If you were hired here, what would you do on your first day?

221: Have you viewed our company's website?

222: How does *X experience* on your resume relate to this position?

223: Why do you want this position?

224: How is your background relevant to this position?

225: How do you feel about *X mission* of our company?

Some of the following titles might also be handy:

1. NET Interview Questions You'll Most Likely Be Asked
2. Access VBA Programming Interview Questions You'll Most Likely Be Asked
3. Adobe ColdFusion Interview Questions You'll Most Likely Be Asked
4. Advanced C++ Interview Questions You'll Most Likely Be Asked
5. Advanced Excel Interview Questions You'll Most Likely Be Asked
6. Advanced JAVA Interview Questions You'll Most Likely Be Asked
7. Advanced SAS Interview Questions You'll Most Likely Be Asked
8. AJAX Interview Questions You'll Most Likely Be Asked
9. Algorithms Interview Questions You'll Most Likely Be Asked
10. Android Development Interview Questions You'll Most Likely Be Asked
11. Ant & Maven Interview Questions You'll Most Likely Be Asked
12. Apache Web Server Interview Questions You'll Most Likely Be Asked
13. Artificial Intelligence Interview Questions You'll Most Likely Be Asked
14. ASP.NET Interview Questions You'll Most Likely Be Asked
15. Automated Software Testing Interview Questions You'll Most Likely Be Asked
16. Base SAS Interview Questions You'll Most Likely Be Asked
17. BEA WebLogic Server Interview Questions You'll Most Likely Be Asked
18. C & C++ Interview Questions You'll Most Likely Be Asked
19. C# Interview Questions You'll Most Likely Be Asked
20. CCNA Interview Questions You'll Most Likely Be Asked
21. Cloud Computing Interview Questions You'll Most Likely Be Asked
22. Computer Architecture Interview Questions You'll Most Likely Be Asked
23. Computer Networks Interview Questions You'll Most Likely Be Asked
24. Core JAVA Interview Questions You'll Most Likely Be Asked
25. Data Structures & Algorithms Interview Questions You'll Most Likely Be Asked
26. EJB 3.0 Interview Questions You'll Most Likely Be Asked
27. Entity Framework Interview Questions You'll Most Likely Be Asked
28. Fedora & RHEL Interview Questions You'll Most Likely Be Asked
29. Hadoop BIG DATA Interview Questions You'll Most Likely Be Asked
30. Hibernate, Spring & Struts Interview Questions You'll Most Likely Be Asked
31. HR Interview Questions You'll Most Likely Be Asked
32. HTML, XHTML and CSS Interview Questions You'll Most Likely Be Asked
33. HTML5 Interview Questions You'll Most Likely Be Asked
34. IBM WebSphere Application Server Interview Questions You'll Most Likely Be Asked
35. iOS SDK Interview Questions You'll Most Likely Be Asked
36. Java / J2EE Design Patterns Interview Questions You'll Most Likely Be Asked
37. Java / J2EE Interview Questions You'll Most Likely Be Asked
38. JavaScript Interview Questions You'll Most Likely Be Asked
39. JavaServer Faces Interview Questions You'll Most Likely Be Asked
40. JDBC Interview Questions You'll Most Likely Be Asked
41. jQuery Interview Questions You'll Most Likely Be Asked
42. JSP-Servlet Interview Questions You'll Most Likely Be Asked
43. JUnit Interview Questions You'll Most Likely Be Asked
44. Linux Interview Questions You'll Most Likely Be Asked
45. Linux System Administrator Interview Questions You'll Most Likely Be Asked
46. Mac OS X Lion Interview Questions You'll Most Likely Be Asked
47. Mac OS X Snow Leopard Interview Questions You'll Most Likely Be Asked
48. Microsoft Access Interview Questions You'll Most Likely Be Asked
49. Microsoft Powerpoint Interview Questions You'll Most Likely Be Asked
50. Microsoft Word Interview Questions You'll Most Likely Be Asked

51. MySQL Interview Questions You'll Most Likely Be Asked
52. Networking Interview Questions You'll Most Likely Be Asked
53. OOPS Interview Questions You'll Most Likely Be Asked
54. Operating Systems Interview Questions You'll Most Likely Be Asked
55. Oracle Database Administration Interview Questions You'll Most Likely Be Asked
56. Oracle E-Business Suite Interview Questions You'll Most Likely Be Asked
57. ORACLE PL/SQL Interview Questions You'll Most Likely Be Asked
58. Perl Programming Interview Questions You'll Most Likely Be Asked
59. PHP Interview Questions You'll Most Likely Be Asked
60. Python Interview Questions You'll Most Likely Be Asked
61. RESTful JAVA Web Services Interview Questions You'll Most Likely Be Asked
62. SAP HANA Interview Questions You'll Most Likely Be Asked
63. SAS Programming Guidelines Interview Questions You'll Most Likely Be Asked
64. Selenium Testing Tools Interview Questions You'll Most Likely Be Asked
65. Silverlight Interview Questions You'll Most Likely Be Asked
66. Software Repositories Interview Questions You'll Most Likely Be Asked
67. Software Testing Interview Questions You'll Most Likely Be Asked
68. SQL Server Interview Questions You'll Most Likely Be Asked
69. Tomcat Interview Questions You'll Most Likely Be Asked
70. UML Interview Questions You'll Most Likely Be Asked
71. Unix Interview Questions You'll Most Likely Be Asked
72. UNIX Shell Programming Interview Questions You'll Most Likely Be Asked
73. Windows Server 2008 R2 Interview Questions You'll Most Likely Be Asked
74. XLXP, XSLT, XPATH, XFORMS & XQuery Interview Questions You'll Most Likely Be Asked
75. XML Interview Questions You'll Most Likely Be Asked

For complete list visit

www.vibrantpublishers.com